"Soul Work"

A Chapbook of Poetry

Elizabeth Spring

DEDICATION

This book is dedicated
To the Seeker in
Each One of Us
And
To that
Which Seeks Us

CONTENTS

1   On Becoming Red   Pg # 1

2   Wild With Words   Pg # 3

3   Back When Pluto Was a Planet   Pg # 5

4   Traversing the Underworld   Pg # 7

5   Soul Work   Pg # 9

6   The Comfort of Words   Pg # 11

7   At My Age   Pg # 13

8   Circa 1833   Pg # 15

9   The Landscape Painter   Pg # 16

10 In the Landscape of the Spirit.   Pg # 18

11 Holy Admiration.   Pg # 21

12 Aging Infrastructure   Pg # 23

13 Shaking Off the Blues.   Pg # 24

14 Old Photographs.   Pg # 26

15. An Old Lover Returns   Pg# 28

17 My Mother's Hollyhocks   Pg # 30

18 Mind-less Love   Pg # 32

19 Choose Again   Pg # 34

20 Tour of Her House   Pg # 37

22 Spirits   Pg # 40

23 The Geometry of the Soul   Pg # 42

24 Fever   Pg # 44

25 Venus Conjunct Pluto   Pg # 46

26 Packing for a Journey Alone   Pg# 49

27 Sarah   Pg # 50

28 Buttons   Pg # 52

29 And Still We Sing Hallelujah.   Pg # 54

1. ON BECOMING RED

As I passed the mirror today
I turned, paused and looked
Not at the wrinkles on my face
Or the heavy hung eyes
But instead—my hair—
Framing my face
Like an old brown frame
On a crackled painting
Revealing a vagueness of look
With the values muted
The hues understated.

And I remembered how
It's been said
That at seventy-four
One is in the "youth of old age"
I never thought about that—
But I did know
In that instant—

That the composition and color
Needed to be changed
The values needed to be deepened
The edges brought out, hard and soft—

"I will become Red!" I grinned—
Dye my hair the color of autumn leaves—
Wear flagrant yellow-greens
And shocking purples

Go out with a burst of color
Before I fall…
So that when I pass that mirror again
I will see the autumn of my life
Written across my face…

And perhaps I'll have red wine at sunset
And drink in the November skies
Till I'm saturated with color
All reds and oranges
And silhouetted
Like the bone-black trees against the skies
Our arms reaching for heaven
Our last leaves bravely waving good-by…

And I will drink till my face is as red
As my hair
And I will write bad poetry—
And read it to my friends
Until they too
Are ready to become Red.

***

2. WILD WITH WORDS

Yesterday I ate berries
Till their blueness spilled out onto my lips as
Thunderstorms threatened with ominous rumbles...

Yesterday I placed my hand to the easel
Pencil and rulers measuring the topography of the land;
The angles, midsection and division of the landscape
Creating perfect order.
Yesterday I ground the cobalt and cerulean blues
Into the sky with the side of my fingers--
Such powerful hands pushing and pressing
The chalky colors
Squashing the pigments and blending the grasses
Moving mountains in olive greens and burnt sienna
Reinforcing the darks with the heal of my hand
I leaned hard into the shadows
Splitting apart the pastel particles onto the paper
Blowing errant crystals away—
Wild with creation
Inhaling the richness of such a colorful impress;
Sloppy with joy.

Until I could taste the cobalt upon my lips
And feel the crimson burn across my eyes
Eyelids now sumptuously closing
Hands raw, nerves prickling—
My burning face, red
Puffed up with signs of a greater tragedy.

Now—such fear—what could have done this?
A bit of undigested cheese or rotted blueberry?
How could I not know?
No…
Passion had turned against me--
Paints rebelled against my hubris—
Poisoning me
Pressing their toxic pigments
Deep into face, lungs, eyes…

Hollow now
As I put the colors away
I think of years of play
Never to be repeated
Wondering
If I might someday
Paint again upon a gentler canvas…
Not as a painter, but as a poet
Wild with words.

***

3. BACK WHEN PLUTO WAS A PLANET

Back when Pluto was a planet
And the Harmonic Convergence
Was known as an auspicious alignment
I became an astrologer.

Back when one's life work
Was more of a choice
Than a challenge and
Love just happened
When Venus aligned with Mars,
Answered questions.

Back when the Soul's trajectory
Across the heavens
Was as significant as knowing if Venus
was the morning or evening star
At the moment of birth—
And "if he loved me or loved me not"
Was not a matter of diminishing flower petals
The stars spoke through me.

Back when the perennial story
Of the Heavens was writ large
Across the sky
And Pluto wasn't questioning his identity—
It mattered what I knew.

But now I say
"The truth, the whole truth
Only comes in shades of gray
And the possibilities
Of paradoxes abound—
In transits, trines and squares…"
And so…
They listen intently
And still they want to know
The answers
To all their questions
The answers
They already know.

***

4. TRAVERSING THE UNDERWORLD

You don't want to be here.
I don't need to explain to you
The ragged geography of the Soul
Other than to say
In these parts
There is no sure footing.
Confidence, even born from experience,
Falls away, and
Hubris is punished.

You may have visited these lands at one time
Our guide, Pluto, Lord of the Underworld,
Wears an invisible mask—
He shines no light—
But lets us fall
Over our own feet
By our naivete, attachments
Possessions, obsessions…
Here, we are not who we were,
But who we are becoming.

As we traverse these rugged lands
We strengthen…
Building Soul
Invisibly—Not by hope—
Because hope would be hope
For the wrong thing—

But by knowing,
As in dying, there is only one password:
Surrender
One action:
Letting go
One choice:
Keeping the Heart open—
Allowing the rebirth
To happen at journey's end—

Allowing the shimmering plumes
Of the phoenix to shock us—
Blinding us to the old world
As we open
To the Numinous Light.

***

5. SOUL WORK

Let us give thanks for the work we do
Let us pay homage to the gods, goddesses,
Symbols, signs and synchronicities
That make their appearance as Grace
When the choice is made "to ask and then to receive"
When "Called or not called, God is present."

Let us give thanks for the chance to be messengers
And guides
To bring the good news that all is well
And all manner of things are well
That life has meaning
That there is a rhyme and reason
A warp and a woof, an inner and an outer
An "As above, so below"
For all god's creatures.

Let us give thanks for this knowledge
That grows into wisdom
That honors life cycles as well as the season's cycles
That sees meaning where others see despair
That sees patterns where others see chaos
That sees hope and evolution where others
See none.

Let us give thanks for ancient soul languages
That challenge us to find the words to translate
The subtle geometry of the Soul
A language that sees

Little acts of change as large acts of courage
That delights at seeing the shy smile of recognition
When the personal story meets the larger story
And is truly heard.

Let us give thanks for Soul Work
That repeatedly shows us how wrong we may be
That what we see first
is not all there is to people—
For we are all richer, more complex
And nobler than we imagine…
And that what we see as God or human flaw
is flawless in design.

Always remembering that the gift is in the effort
And in the practice of reaching to understand
This Soul Work, and all the unknowable mysteries
For which we are so truly grateful.

***

6. THE COMFORT OF WORDS

Retreating from the cold blue light
Of this New Year's Day
I wander through the house
Seeking refuge from the cool liminal spaces
To rest in the cozy spot near the window.
Here the salmon-colored walls, golden light,
And deep shadows reside…
Here I've come to be held—
Papers pen, pillows
A cup of tea in hand.

All morning I worked to clear a space, a place
For the comfort of words.
Now it is done: the slow ordering of familiar objects:
The old chair cleared of its pile of books,
The cobalt blue canisters aligned like a row of children
The desk relieved of its weight of papers.

The clearing brought a peace—or at least a cautious truce
Between the never-ending disarray of chaos
And the promise of that clear new slate.
And this I have done before.
I have cleared away and begun anew.

But now as I rest in this afternoon light
I recall how I have always paused
To clear spaces—how I have readied myself
To leap again into uncertain beginnings
How I have braced against necessary endings

And shuddered at inevitable choices, but still
I have risked all, for dreams.

Looking around the room
The yet undusted objects speak to me—
My old friends: the antique clock
The brown clay bowl,
The amber lamp.
Even the shoes that are now too tight…
Must these be let go of--?
To make way for what?
I take my pen in hand
Seeking answers;
seeking the comfort of words.

Beginnings demand endings
As birth demands death
Yet today I remain curiously in-between worlds
I'm not ready to release; let go. Begin anew.
I will wait.
Closing my eyes, I drift…
My hand clenching and unclenching the pen…
While I sink into finer works,
Where timelessness,
Like the gently falling dust and snow,
Covers me, as I give way…
To the comfort of words.

***

7. AT MY AGE

Staring down at my morning coffee
Steaming in the clay mug
Gives me more pleasure
Then eye-ing
The "days of the week" pill box
With its unspoken air of authority
To "forget me not."

At my age
I don't like its implications
Of "shoulds and should nots"
And the memories
Of how they got there.

At our age, who has not felt
The fright of a suspicious lump—
Or the pressure of a heart sputtering;
Beating to its uncontrolled rhythm
Or the unwelcome fatigue
Of a body needing to retire mid-day.
There's got to be a pill
For all of that.

At my age
First thing in the morning
I'd rather sit and watch the birds
Twitching with excitement
At the feeder
Or speculate about what the dog
Might be thinking
As she flies through the air

Catching the one thing
she loves the most,
second only to me,
And her dry kibble.

I want to live into the day ahead
Like these creatures
Un-encumbered
By the necessities and vicissitudes
Of age
And to yet again discover
The one thing I love the most

Or at least to sit in my chair,
With eyes closed
Simply dreaming
Of what that might be…
And then, only then,
To open the box
Of the "Day's Daily Requirements."

***

8 CIRCA 1833

When part of the ceiling fell down
Yesterday
Without provocation
I was astounded.
But then again
Old houses and old bodies
Fall apart
Without provocation.

It was then my mind fell upon
The words
Omen and *ominous*
Wondering if they might be related
And how unannounced it all was
Like the moment
I spotted the ruins
Of what was once our bedroom ceiling
On the floor
While walking down the hall
Between mid-life and old age.

***

9. THE LANDSCAPE PAINTER

As if for the first time
I taste the sweetness
Of ripening.

As if for the first time
My fingers scumble blueness
Across the scratchy paper...
My hands press
The powdered sticks of color
Into the sky—
A streak of yellow—
A shout of orange—
An exclamation of white—
Until God peaks out through the clouds
Breaking through cliches
Of thought and habit
As if for the first time.

As if for the first time
The earth demands the darks
Of eggplant purples and crimson burgundies
Their deep values undisputed;
They must be first!
They are the ground of the earth.
Then the dry chalks of lighter colors
Begin to blend
Into creamy lavenders

And robin egg blues
As moonlit nights
Shimmer with light
And luminosity.

As if for the first time
I show up at the easel
Pushing and pulling
With parched hands,
Trying to create a world
Eleven by fourteen—
And I will try again
And again…
Showing up
Till magic happens…
For I can taste the sweetness
Of ripening.

***

10   IN THE LANDSCAPE OF THE SPIRIT

"Paint the mountains blue" my teacher said
For the atmosphere of distance
Is always soft and blue.

So far away, like a dream forgotten, I thought.
Yes, kind of blue...
Like you and I
Songs are sung in blues
For in the landscape of the Spirit—
In the distance from our hearts—
Is always a hint of blue.

He went on:
The secret of the landscape
(Which only the Masters knew)
Was to put a dot of red
At the end of the curve in the road
Just beyond the line of trees
In the space one can't see—
Making us curious
As to what lies beyond.

And...at sunrise and sunset
Paint a line of yellow and orange
With a streak of rose at the horizon—
That's where "the radiance" breaks through...
Then, lead the eye still higher...
Until you merge
Into the ethereal blueness

Of the sky...
It's the atmosphere of distance
He repeated.
It's always blue, I thought.

And what about green? I complained—
It's always the greens
We remember...
Thinking of how
In and out of lifetimes
It's the 'greenness" that pulls us back
From blue, pushing its way
Through the gray stones of winter and frozen hope
The tiniest shoots of mossy grass
Returning to cover all
In slightly altered states
We return to heal and love again.

"Yes, put in the greens!" he said
For the atmosphere of intimacy
Is always green in the landscape of the heart
It's the dream remembered—
So, paint the foregrounds green.

Yet—I protested still—pastel in hand—
What about the purple-pinks with dashes of turquoise
Scumbled across the thirsty paper?
Aren't these God's colors too?
I was thinking about this morning's walk
And the white heron's graceful landing
Across the misty pond—
The deep rich indigo of the wild iris...
Remembering it all.

"Yes, yes, you must paint it all—
The wide expanse of Soul, and more!"
His large hands expressing
What he could not put in words…
He knew my thoughts…
I could not do what he did.
"I know, I know, I said,
Then laughed
"I got it, Boss—
I got it."

***

11 HOLY ADMIRATION

The way the hydrangeas
Raise their heads in the morning
After being defeated by yesterday's midday sun
Never ceases to amaze me.

And the way the old dog
So large and arthritic
So languorously
Glides along
On his morning walk—
In squelching heat—
Never ceases to
Make me wonder
About his Buddhahood.

But the way
I rise out of bed
After a sleepless night
And manage to smile at you
Sitting in the kitchen—
So eager for your day—
Fills me
With holy admiration
For the nobility

Of my intentions
And the possible duplicity
Of my heart.

***

12.   AGING INFRASTRUCTURE

This morning
As I rose from my bed
Exhausted
From yet another restless night
Of Alice in Wonderland journeys…
I made the coffee
Attempted pleasant conversation
And walked the dog…
All the while wondering
About the infamous Mark Twain
And how he pushed on through the barriers
Of time, energy and sorrow
To carry on despite lagging spirits…
Leaving this earth
As he predicted—
With the equally infamous
Halley's Comet.

"It is better to wear out
Than to rust out" he is quoted as saying,
And though I am tired
I will take his words to heart
And push on
Despite this failing infra-structure…
Or until some un-auspicious planetary alignment
Or shooting asteroid
Takes me out
Not as a dying ember—
But in a blaze of fire—
As I move on
To yet another world.
***

13. SHAKING OFF THE BLUES

Sitting in the red armchair
Staring at the late afternoon light dancing
Upon the weathered tree
I admire the tenacious leaves
Clinging to home still
Shaking and shivering till
They each fall
Still hoping to last forever
Or at least till spring.

And I catch myself—
Remembering the person
I once was
Barely rooted
Loosely connected to all
And yearning to stay with those
Who would not fall
Those whose leaves shown bright
With color
Desperately to see myself
Through the eyes of another
Fleeing from the ravages time would bring
Fleeing from the loneliness
The winters came and went
And still I remained
Though many did not...

Now sitting here
Pen in hand
I pour the wine,
play the old songs

Write the poem…

Grateful for feeling deeply rooted
in this life I've built—
attached to the Whole—
while
watching the Light
Shimmer across the surface
Of the Pinot Noir
As it slides down the side
Of the over-flowing glass…
Shaking off the blues.

***

14. OLD PHOTOGRAPHS

There I am in the café,
sitting in front of the potted geraniums
wearing the straw hat I just bought.
I was writing a postcard to my mother
When I looked up to see the shadows
Of the early autumn evening
Dancing across the stucco walls.

Then you walked by—
You were taking pictures of the light—
I watched you
trying to imagine what you were seeing there
And then you turned your gaze on me
And shot this one here—
A little out of focus—
but it was then that I saw them
The tenderest eyes I'd ever seen.

Look. This is where we found ourselves standing later
By the edge of the river
The one Van Gogh painted
We walked for hours feeling the night air
You talked apertures, lens and focus.

This was the hotel, Le D'Arlatan…
Do you remember wandering the back streets
Lost in the cobbled labyrinths
Till we found ourselves here?

The oversized antique bed held expectations.
I felt shy
You said "Pull the curtains"
and I pulled the heavy curtains back.
I read you a poem by candlelight
You smiled right into my soul
Then served us farmer's wine
In the opalescent glasses we'd bought that day.

I put the photographs down.
"It was so good," you say,
"Like the wisp of a dream I can barely remember."
I lean into your eyes; those milky apertures
Transparent with the film of a lifetime.

Now, I offer you wine and pull the curtains open
Catching the last dance of light on the peach-colored walls.
You put on the old songs…
We sit in chairs by the window,
Admiring the blue hydrangeas
Our knees will touch
and we will speak about how
the quality of light makes everything different
and everything the same.

***

15.   AN OLD LOVER RETURNS

You came back into my life yesterday
Somehow, you found
that small window of opportunity
Left open
By this tired bruised heart of mine
You touched me so sweetly
I could not resist
Yes, yes, I said. Yes, I would give you the world.
And then you left.
Yes…perhaps I forgot…
You; a lunar watery creature
Whose blue eyes
And elusive tender ways enchant me…
Perhaps I forgot the undertow of your seaweed
entanglements
Those ghosts who pull you to your underworld life
Where bodies and emotions swim and drown themselves
Into sweet amnesia.
And tonight, I remain here on this dry land
Perched and left on this rock
Like Psyche…waiting…waiting…
I ask: Eros, where are you? Where are you?
Unfortunately I know where you are.

Is this an omen I ask?
Or am I some isolated solar star
Unnamed, uncharted, playing with yet
Another unrealistic fantasy conjured up

In some early morning reverie?

Tell me—are there any true changes
We can make?
Any new adventures to take?
Or are there only tender teachings
That bruise the heart into opening?
I can only stand on the shore, wait,
And keep faith.

***

16. MY MOTHER'S HOLLYHOCKS

At eighty-five, my mother didn't have
The English cottage garden
Nor did she have the hollyhocks
But she loved these flowers
And painted them in oils…
And I, her only daughter
Only cursorily said:
"How nice" they were
More astonished by her age
Than her art.

Now "nice" isn't a nice word
Connotating instead an insipid approval:
Uninspired, uncourageous
Or perhaps implying even trite.
Though I didn't take the time
To even think of that.

And now at seventy-five, I don't have
The English cottage garden either
Nor do I have the hollyhocks
But I have her painting
And I will paint them too.
Yet my hollyhocks will now be hers
Copied meticulously~
And each stroke
Of her radiant petal blossoms
And wide leafed greens

Will now be mine…
And I will wonder too, as perhaps she did
If my only daughter will like it too
and hope~
With all my heart
That my mother will now know
That her painting was truly good
And that tearfully, and finally
I took the time
To truly look, to admire,
And to trace the contours
Of her heart on mine.

***

17.   Mind-less Love

Do you remember the day—
It was New Year's day I believe—
When we sat in the kitchen
Listening to some old folk song
On the radio
While I was sewing buttons
On some raggedy old bear
To make eyes
And you were repairing a torn off limb
The puppy had mangled
While she now
Lay sleeping at your feet...

And I turned to you to ask
What you wanted...
I meant in life
At this moment of our life...
And you replied:
"A cup of tea with honey
Would be nice."
And I laughed.

The day was cold, gray and wet
A staple of New England this time of year
But a cup of tea with honey for you
And a glass of wine for me
Would keep away the blues
Letting time

Slip away
Like unknotted threads
Sewn through button holes
A thread that would never hold
But a love
That would never cease.

***

18. Choose Again

As I lie in bed this morning
Loosely pondering the motivation
To awake or remain motionless…
I float between worlds, wandering lightly
Amid some nuance of a half-forgotten dream
Rising from that other world.

I am…the beach. It is hot.
The ocean rolls over me
I don't think I remember how to swim.

Yet…I am no longer in that other world
I am instead in this familiar dream
I call my life.
It shouldn't be so easy to get lost here
Or drown.

I open my eyes
Squinting at the fragments of my life
Strewn around the room—
Sweaters thrown in corners
Shoes tossed beside the bed
White sheets of paper slithering
Across the desk
Precipitously close to the edge…
When the unbidden voices
Of uncertainty, critique, and obligation
Crash in upon me, forcing

Beads of water across my forehead.

I rise in the gray twilight
Of this September morn
And wonder—what will I find today?
A lost ring among the sweaters?
A forgotten place to go to among the shoes?
A lost syllable of my life
Dropped among the papers?
What forgotten piece of my true nature
--what Zen particle—
Might I find under the stack of books?

I step outside the kitchen door
To meet another world
Where the gently moving morning air
Caresses my skin
And the chatter of birdsong quiets the night's fear.

Here the world prepares herself
Fresh for a new day
Stirring my Soul
With such kind remembrances of a softer life—
Distracting and seducing it
From its long night-journey home.

Here in the garden
The grasses and flowers hold no grievance
Nor tell troubled tales of what transpired
During the night: the deer that wandered through the yard
The nesting creatures that tunneled
Through the earth

Here there is no worry
Whether sun or rain will shorten life
Or what wild weed is taking over.

Here the nostalgia of the mint
And the mystery of the wide-leafed weed
Dissolve this morning's melancholy
Like the amber tea
Brewing in the pot…
Its pungent fragrance awakening a
Deeper well of memory.

The night dreams have passed.
I will not drown.
And as the morning mist
Lifts the quiet sorrow
That steeped my Soul
In shades of gray
Gives way to this pearly dawn
I rejoice—
As night dreams
Become day dreams—
And I choose again
Which story to live today.

***

19. TOUR OF HER HOUSE

Here's where her sweater hangs
On its hook
And here's where she sleeps

She eats here
And naps there

You see, her name is on her dish
There
And she rests in the courtyard
There
Always there...
Under that tree.

They say she's not here
Anymore.
She's there.
Where the bone is
Where the flowers are
Where the dirt is loose
In the courtyard
Where she rests under the tree.

Where is she?
They say she's there
Could you show me
Where there is, please?
I can't see
I don't understand.

20. GOING TO THE LAVENDER FARM

I picture it differently
Sunny, a few wisps of clouds
Cerulean blue skies
Painted across the canvas...
The distant farmhouse
A spot of red
The longish grasses bending slightly
The picnic basket overflowing.

But we are here now
Under a cloudy sky
With a litany of expectations
Yet it is good.

We are in that French painting
By Manet, I think
Or perhaps it was a different painter
You, in your long white skirt
Me, in something flowing
Impressionistic...
Languorously
Stretched across the quilt
Telling a story...
"Toujours jolie."

I will read from my book of poetry
You will pour the wine.
I will bring my "joie de vivre"

We will laugh.

We are here now
Under this lavender gray sky
On your seventieth birthday,
Dear one
And it is good.
Pour me a glass
Of your pink champagne
And we will
Breathe in the scent
Of lavender fields forever...

***

21. SPIRITS

I left the window open
Last night
And returning home late
Saw my light still on
In the window.
And to my surprise
The rain had come in
Splattering my painting—
Leaving the half that got rained on
With such a beautiful pattern—
The angular lines softened
The colors bleeding into one another
I gasped; looked around—

The amber light on the table
Spilled into the shadows
Warming the room
While the tired sun sent
Quivering patterns
Of pine branches against the walls
Hinting of some feral ghost
Come and gone—
The books strewn across the floor
Blown open by some ferocious wind
Beckoned me to read their open pages
Holding secrets from authors
Long since gone.

What grace was this?
I only know
When the world wearies
And ceases to satisfy
I turn towards home and
To the Mysteries
And memories
Of these rooms...
Knowing I am not alone.

***

22. THE GEOMETRY OF THE SOUL

How does one write a poem?
How does one summon the muse
To decipher
The geometry of the Soul?

These were the questions I pondered
As I sat there
Pen in hand
Staring at the sunlit shadows
Darting across the dirty window pane...
I might be more inclined
To clean it
Rather than to just sit here
And stare
As poets must do
Unmoving
Except for the persistent pondering
Of the impossibility of inspiration
And the quiet wisdom of the cat
Sitting on the window sill
Un-twitching—
In her Zen like state.

But the poet's job is to delve
Not to do, to clean or fix anything
Or even to take the dog for a walk
So I can only sit, wait and marvel
At my lack of wit or wisdom
Arising from deep within.

And so I sit, unmoved.

Un-defined in all degrees
I pause and resist the wordy propensity to preach
Or to fall into the ditch of sentimentality
But simply to persist; pen in hand
This solitary pursuit
Scribbling lines that will never meet in space
Nor finding the right angle to resolve the tension
But simply knowing that stillness
Is the singular point of challenge
For the poet—
And that the geometry of the Soul
Is an equation
That cannot be summed by will.

***

23. FEVER

First I felt it in my knees
A peculiar weakness
And then that particular chill
Of heat rising within

Fearing to faint
I rushed to take cover
In the soft cave
Of bed covers
Curling up like a fetus
And began watching
The curious cinema
Of my life
Unveil behind closed eyes.

Not unpleasant—
Such vivid images arose:
Once more I am a little girl
My father's eyes smiling at me
As he tucks me in
Strokes my head
Placing the wet cold cloth of childhood
Across my forehead.

And then there was the tour—
The virtual reality
Of all the rooms of my life
I need only turn my eyes to catch
Each singular detail
Redolent with meaning:

The gold statue of Jesus on the shelf
Beneath the Golden-book Series
Of childhood books...
And the mirror on the far wall
Reflecting the face of a girl
Who didn't know who she was.

And now—what cloistered retreat
Was I being called to here?
A life review; a feverish journey?
My knees, my will,
Still failing
I slept...
And seem to fall
Into something
Larger than myself
Held by invisible hands
And some unknown
Workings of grace,
I surrendered
To a bright
Falling
Upwards.

***

24. VENUS CONJUNCT PLUTO

Tonight—at sunset—I went down
To the bottom of the boat.
Steel doors locking behind me
Descending into his darkness
I boarded this boat, death place of fish—
What did I hope for here?

Enclosed, trapped, dark
Nothing alive survives here—
Why must I play out these feral illusions?
This siren call—
Storm tossed and wild—
Curious
I'd set the bait myself.
He found my note, frozen
in the bottom of a barrel.
Come visit, he said, and I did.

He sits me down next to the helm
Overlooking the bay,
Looming large here
He looks hard, wounded
A bloodied hand from too much work
"It's all I know" he says.

He tells me how in a storm he goes slow, drifts—
Rolls with the waves, and likes it.
This I like.
Whereas I go too fast—

Too passionate, I knock myself off course
Making me homesick, seasick—
Losing myself.

Eyeing me now, he wonders why I've come
Some flight of fancy he thinks—
Or worse—
Some flight of desperation
I know.

"Our work is similar I say:
We set the bait and hope to catch the fish"
I pause and smile.
"There's a difference," he says
"I go out and net them—
You lure them in."
He smiled
Through stained teeth.
I shivered.

The light was dimming
A narrow pink strip of hope
Appeared along the horizon.
"Where's Venus?" I said
Knowing she was nowhere near here
Where were the words to hide?
How far off course I'd come…

Silence descended. He shifted in his seat
And looked full-square at me
He spoke of how a man went down to hell
To save his woman—
"Persephone" I argued,
"Was abducted into hell—

What heroic expectations
Were getting washed out here?
Would I, who had come to see—
Too curious—
Find myself hooked and writing
On these dank wooden floors?
"Would you like a cookie?" he asked.
Fear.
"I must get home before dark," I said,
I must get home before dark—

***

25. PACKING FOR A JOURNEY ALONE

I buy a necklace
Of colored buttons
Red, purple, green—
A collage of buttons
Strung with fragile threads.
"They'll break easily" I say
To the clerk as if she cared;
Fear in my voice.
"But they're friendly" she says.
"It's inviting conversation," I reply
"Like talking about unexpected treasures
Found in an old sewing box."
But I know
It's a string
Of little shields
Ritually protecting me
From the critical eyes
Of strangers.

***

26. SARAH

She was so beautiful there—
Sitting wrapped in the white woolen shawl
Enveloping her bare shoulders
Her long purple peasant dress
Flowing around her delicate feet.

I wanted to take a photograph
To capture the moment,
Thinking she could never be more beautiful that this
Pregnant, young, in love.
How could I capture the moment?

But I hesitated…
One shouldn't make an event
Out of every ordinary moment—
But this moment; this moment in time—
My heart bursting, eyes overflowing
Nothing had prepared me for this.

What courage was emerging from within!
From she who was being born,
And she who was birthing.

If only I could place
A cloak of protection
Around her—
Work some wise-women ways—
Offer more sustenance, more courage
Though of course, she needed nothing

Now, all I can give is a poem.
But then, all I could do was simply
Take off my necklace
And lay it gently around her neck
Crowning her with all my mother-love.

***

27. BUTTONS

Following the threads
Of chosen words
One crafts a life
As one crafts a tapestry;
Following the threads
Of small acts of choice
And courage
Raveling and unraveling
The particulars of a life
Following the story-line home.

Catching hold of a purple thread of sorrow
A yellow line of joy
I needle through the cloth,
Buttoning together the places of the heart
That must be bound
Knurly and knotted; piecing and stringing
Such fragile threads
I hide the back-side from view.
"Such a beautiful piece they say, "strung together
By such rich, colorful threads."

Yet I know how I suffered the broken threads—
The illusions, false engagements, subtle betrayals—
So much paradox and possibility;
At times, the fabric barely held.

For far too long
I'd look at the torn places

And sewed
Through button-eyes
Unknotted
They released themselves—
As I sought to make connections
that were not mine to make.

But now the needle moves rhythmically
Through the holy quartet
Of a single button
I see how the parts relate
How the singular threads
Need to be knotted and interwoven
Buttoned with the belief
That there are meaningful patterns
In this life...
The stitches are beginning to hold;
The torn places are mending.

Slowly and persistently
The heart cries out—
And what needs to become attached,
Attaches—
And what needs to become detached
Detaches—
But nothing gets thrown away...
As I've become a keeper of buttons.

***

28. AND STILL WE SING HALLULUJAH

The girl
Rose from the pew
And took a stand
In the center
Of the chapel
And sang.

So young, so alone!
So unaccompanied in song and life—
We sang every chorus with her—
As if we could lift her up
Above it all—
And save her.
Our throats choking
Tears falling
Hearts opening.

The innocent and the mundane
The sacred and the profane…
The lyrics struck a chord
Resonating
From one Elder's acceptance of defeat
Despair and perhaps redemption…
Down through the family of man
To her, and to us…
And still
In the face of it all—
We sing
One broken "Hallelujah."

Elizabeth Spring, MA, has a degree in psychology with an emphasis in the work of Carl Jung. She has used this degree as an astrological counselor and has written six books. She has been a poet all her life, as well as a potter and painter. The mother of one daughter, and grandmother to two grand-daughters, she lives in Wickford Village in Rhode Island where she and her husband, Harry, run Spring Pottery Gallery, where they sell their pottery and paintings. She can also be reached at: ElizabethSpring@aol.com

Made in the USA
Middletown, DE
14 October 2022

12749845R00038